Golf Rules Made

A Practical Guide to the Rules Most Frequently Encountered on the Golf Course

Written by
John Gregory

All rights reserved. No part of this book may be reproduced or transmitted in any form or by any means, electronic or mechanical, including photocopying, recording or by any information storage or retrieval system, without permission in writing from the publisher.

Contents

INTRODUCTION	8
A SELF-POLICING GAME	8
FROM ANCIENT TO MODERN RULES	10
WHY LEARN THE RULES?	11
CHAPTER 1 – Pre-tee off	14
LOCAL RULES	14
PRE-MATCH CHECKLIST	15
MATCHPLAY OR STROKEPLAY?	15
HANDICAPPING	16
STROKE INDEX	17
CHAPTER 2 – Playing by the rules off the 1st	18
TEEING OFF TIPS	18
PLAY IT AS IT LIES	19
TENDING THE FLAG	20
CHAPTER 3 – Provisional play on the 2nd	22
TEEING GROUND TACTICS	22
PROVISIONAL BALL/ FIVE-MINUTE RULE	23
CALLING THROUGH	24
ESSENTIAL PUTTING GREEN RULES	25
CHAPTER 3 – Out of Bounds	27
SLICING OUT OF BOUNDS	27
BALL KNOCKED OFF TEE	27
A FREE DROP	28
ON HAZARDOUS GROUND	28

RAKING THE BUNKER 29

CHAPTER 5 –Water 30

    WATER HAZARD PROCEDURE 30

    BALL DAMAGE..31

CHAPTER 6 - The Long 5th - The Long Search 32

    PRACTISING - THE RULES 32

    ROUGH JUSTICE 33

    WHOSE BALL IS IT ANYWAY? 34

    UNPLAYABLE BALL 35

    HOW AND WHERE TO DROP THE BALL............................36

CHAPTER 7 – Into the Wind on the 6th..................................38

    THERE'S NO SUCH THING AS AN INNOCENT QUESTION....38

    PERFECT TOUCHDOWN - WRONG BASE 40

    TO DROP AGAIN? 40

    THE SPIRIT OR THE LETTER OF THE RULES? 40

CHAPTER 8 – 7th Heaven 42

    ASSISTED PASSAGE 42

    WHAT IS AN OUTSIDE AGENCY? 43

    A WATER SPORT?..43

    OPTIONS OUT OF THE WATER 44

    WILLING THE BALL IN...45

CHAPTER 9 – Rain at the 8th 47

    WRONG TEEING GROUND 47

    A SPORTING GESTURE 48

    CASUAL WATER...48

 SEMI-ROUGH LUCK 49

 'I DIDN'T TOUCH THE BALL!!' 50

 THE RIGHT 'ADDRESS' 50

 BALL DEEMED TO HAVE MOVED 51

 NATURAL IMPEDIMENTS TO NATURAL PLAY 52

 ON YOUR KNEES 52

 MOVING, BENDING, BREAKING 53

 STILL ALL SQUARE 54

CHAPTER 10 – All on the 9th 55

 NEVER RULE OUT THE HAZARDS 55

 GROUND UNDER REPAIR (G.U.R.) 56

 MOVABLE/IMMOVABLE OBSTACLES 56

 SEARCH & RE-COVER 58

 BUNKER DROP 59

 DOUBLE HIT 60

Chapter 11 – To the 19th 62

 MARKING THE SCORECARD 62

 TYPES OF PLAY 63

CHAPTER 12 – Rules Reviewed 65

 DELVING DEEPER INTO THE RULES 65

 MAXIMUM 14 CLUBS 65

 TENDING THE FLAGSTICK 66

 1 OVER 5 MINUTE RULE 66

 LIFTING & MARKING 67

 RE- TEE PENALTY? 68

PITCHMARK PROBLEMS	68
HIDDEN BUNKER HAZARDS	69
WATER HAZARDS	70
UNPLAYABLE BALL	70
ADVICE	71
WILDLIFE RULES OK	71
AS THE CROW FLIES	72
DOWNSTREAM, UPWIND	73
EXERTING INFLUENCE?	73
CASUAL WATER	74
BALL AT REST MOVED	74
LOOSE IMPEDIMENTS	75
IMPROVING LIE OR LINE OF PLAY	75
OBSTRUCTIONS	76
STICKING TO THE RULES	77
ALWAYS MORE TO LEARN	78

INTRODUCTION

Games we play like football, rugby, cricket, or tennis usually have referees, umpires or officials. We don't have to think about the rules. Even if we do need to know them, they are probably fairly easy to understand and there aren't too many of them.

Not so golf. With golf there is no referee or umpire, at least not in an average club tournament. The player is his own referee, calling penalties upon himself if appropriate, even if his opponent would not have known of any breach of the rules. This is the essence of golf, where fair play is the backbone of the game, without the acrimonious disputes so common in other sports today.

A SELF-POLICING GAME

Millions of golfers all over the world appreciate that the 'self-policing' aspect of golf is one reason why it is such an enjoyable, relaxing game, and this is reinforced when they see professional golfers displaying the same attitude of fair play.

But that leaves one problem - how to get to know the rules of golf. Simple, you say: get a rule book and keep it in your golf bag. And indeed you should. The Rules of Golf - the official publication as approved by the Royal and Ancient Golf Club of St Andrews (R&A) and the United States Golf Association (USGA) - sets out the rules of golf (applicable worldwide), is updated every four years and is available free in booklet form.

However, the rules are not easy to understand in isolation and there are too many of them to learn by heart. After all, even professional golfers have to consult the rule book in many instances or call for an official tournament referee to clarify a situation. From the ordinary golfer's point of view, it is undoubtedly more useful to have a reasonable knowledge of the most important rules rather than attempt to have a little knowledge of all of them.

Close encounters with the Common Rules

In Golf Rules, it is the most common and controversial rules, infringements, penalties and points of Etiquette and their practical application on the golf course that are highlighted and explained. In an easy-to-understand format, we follow two representative golfers, John and David, over a sample nine holes that throws at them most of the situations, incidents and hazards - if not the book itself - that call for an on-the-spot understanding and decision on the rules. You can then follow the rules, not as some abstract, legal handing-down-of-committee decisions over 250 years, but as a daily hurdle all golfers out there trying to better their game have to encounter.

FROM ANCIENT TO MODERN RULES

The first rules were actually published in 1744 by the Honourable Company of Edinburgh Golfers (later adopted by The Royal & Ancient Golf Club of St Andrews) and there were just 13 of them. As you can see below, while the basic precepts might be recognizable to today's golfer, the language is a little harder to fathom!

1. You must tee your Ball within a Club Length if the hole.
2. Your tee must be upon the Ground.
3. You are not to Change the ball which you Strike off the Tee.
4. You are not to Remove Stones, Bones or Break Club for the Sake of playing Your Ball Except upon the fair Green and that only within a Club Length if your Ball.
5. If your Ball come among Water, or any Watery filth, You are at Liberty to take your Ball, and throwing it behind the hazard 6 yards at least. You may play it with any Club, and allow your Adversary a Stroke, for so getting out your Ball.
6. If your Balls be found anywhere touching one another, You are to lift the first Ball, till You play the last.
7. At holeing, You are to play your Ball honestly for the Hole, and not play upon your Adversary's Ball, not lying in your way to the hole.
8. If you should lose your Ball, by its being taken up, or any other way, You are to go back to the Spot where you Struck last, and drop another ball, and Allow your adversary a stroke for the Misfortune.
9. No man at holeing his Ball, is to be allowed to Mark his way to the Hole with his Club or anything else.
10. If a Ball be Stop'd by any person, Horse, Dog or anything else, the Ball so Stop'd Must be played where it lyes.
11. If you draw your Club, in Order to Strike, and proceed so far in the Stroke as to be bringing down your Club; if then your Club shall break, in any way, it is to be counted a Stroke.

12. He, Whose Ball lyes furthest from the Hole is Obliged to play first.

13. Neither Trench, Ditch, or Dyke made for the preservation if the Links, Nor the Scholars Holes or the Soldiers Lines, shall be accounted a Hazard, But the Ball is to be taken out, Teed and played with any Iron Club.

WHY LEARN THE RULES?

The basic principles of those first 13 rules can be applied to the modern game but, many would say unfortunately, there are now 34 rules, numerous sub-sections and definitions, taking up over 100 pages of text, in a necessarily legal, dry style, making the task of getting to grips with them comprehensively virtually impossible.

So why bother to try and learn, or play by, the rules at all? Why not just knock the ball around the course making up your own rules as you go along? Won't you be regarded as a nuisance if you are constantly referring to the rules? Not at all: if you play to the rules, then you can enjoy your golf, without spoiling anyone else's, and know that you are going to have a fair game.

So every golfer needs some knowledge of the rules - not encyclopedic - but enough to cover the everyday situations in a round of golf, that you might be playing anywhere in the world, whether with your best golfing friends, or with a complete stranger. It doesn't matter where, when or with whom - you will all be playing to the same rules.

Follow our golfing partners John and David over nine holes of their weekend game and you will certainly feel a lot more confident with a basic knowledge of the most important rules when you step onto the 1st tee.

THE BEGINNER...

For John, the rules were a daunting prospect, given that he was a relative novice to the game. He'd taken up golf just over a year ago at the age of 25 after watching it avidly on TV since a succession of closely fought Ryder Cups had brought golf alive to millions who had previously thought of it as an old man's game.

He had become a regular at his local driving range, practising his swing in the evenings after work, and taking a course of beginners' group lessons which had given him a good basic practical grasp of the game. After six months, he had treated himself to a full set of clubs, some golf shoes and several items of golf gear in the current fashion favoured by the top tournament pros. Luckily for John, there was also a pay-and-play nine hole course nearby, so he had ventured out for the occasional round from time to time. He had a vague inkling about the rules, having noticed that some of the players on the course didn't seem to behave in quite the manner he had seen in the last Open on TV! But come to think of it, neither had he. "Turn up and Tee off" had been the only rule so far.

... AND THE RULES 'BUFF'

David was pleased that John had taken up golf, as he was when he managed to introduce anybody to what he regarded as the game of a lifetime. That day in the office when John had talked about seeing the Ryder Cup on TV had been the turning point. David suggested trying the driving range and taking a course of lessons. When it turned out that John was hooked, David had kept a friendly eye on his progress, joining him at the driving range for the occasional evening practice session.

But they hadn't played golf together yet. David had his regular weekend game at the club he had belonged to for nearly 20 years and where his handicap was currently 11. He had even reached the dizzy heights of a 'single figure' handicap (8) for a brief period, but the pressures of a young family had soon put paid to that. Nevertheless, 11 was very respectable by any standards and David had a pretty thorough knowledge of most aspects of the game, including the rules. Now that John had progressed to the stage of playing on the public course, David thought the least he could do would be to invite him for a game at his club: nine holes on a quiet summer evening would be ideal. A date was fixed, and all was set for the 'friendly' rules-abiding match.

David had suggested that they met in the pro's shop where he would sign him in as his guest. John realized that if he made a good impression at David's local golf club he might eventually achieve one of his ambitions: to be nominated for club membership by David.

CHAPTER 1 – Pre-tee off

The formalities completed, John was ready to face the moment of truth. David gave John a card of the course after he signed him in, and off they went towards the 1st tee.

LOCAL RULES

David mentioned that one of the features of the course was that there were an awful lot of stones in the bunkers. But in the Local Rules printed on the back of the card, you were allowed to remove them before you played your shot. David had given John a useful tip to being forewarned about the rules, and that it must always be worth checking the Local Rules before you start your round.

Local Rules variations covering local conditions, made and published by the Committee of the course in question, can often provide 'relief (such as a free drop away from a fixed sprinkler head) which would not normally be available under the Rules of Golf, and they define areas such as out of bounds, water hazards or ground under repair, which nowadays include 'environmentally-sensitive' areas from which play can be prohibited. All useful information to know in advance so that you can take the right action when necessary with the minimum of fuss and delay.

Useful information such as: 'Safety (cliff edge). A ball coming to rest within two club lengths of the cliff edge at the 14th must be lifted and dropped within three club lengths of the cliff edge without penalty.' You would certainly want to know that rather unnerving local rule at Barton-on-Sea Golf Club, Hampshire, UK. Or if you were playing at Jinja in Uganda, you might want to take advantage of a local rule which allows you to lift your ball from a hippo's footprint without penalty.

John was certain of one thing: he was going to watch David very carefully not just to pick up any tips on the intricacies of the golf swing and the official rules, but also to try and make sure he observed the 'Etiquette' of golf. The simple meaning of Etiquette is a common sense way of behaving so as not to spoil anyone else's game and leaving the course in the condition you'd like to find it. In fact, he noticed one thing straightaway: David didn't take his trolley up on to the tee (as John was about to), but left it on the path next to the tee: obvious, really, the tee would soon get damaged if it constantly had trolleys wheeled over it.

PRE-MATCH CHECKLIST

John rummaged in his bag for a half decent ball (he couldn't remember which pocket he'd put them in – he must get more organized next time) and noticed David was counting his clubs. John suddenly realized that he might be about to break a very basic rule: Maximum of 14 clubs (Rule 4-4). Was that extra wedge that he'd borrowed from his friend at the driving range still in his bag? Yes, it was and that made 15 clubs in all.

After returning the offending wedge quickly to the boot of his car, John checked with David what the penalty would have been. In Matchplay, at the conclusion of the hole at which the breach is discovered, the state of the match is adjusted by deducting one hole for each hole at which a breach occurred, with a maximum deduction of two holes per round. In Strokeplay, a deduction of two strokes per hole at which any breach occurred would apply, with a maximum of four strokes per round.

MATCHPLAY OR STROKEPLAY?

All of which prompted John to ask David whether they were playing Matchplay (Rule 2) or Strokeplay (Rule 3)? In the former, the game is played by holes and a hole is won by the player or side which holes the ball in the fewest strokes. The game is won by the player or side more holes 'up' (ahead) than there are holes left to play. A match can be 'halved' if the match score is 'all square' at the end of the stipulated round. If a win or lose result is required (in a club match, for example), the players would play the '19th' (normally the 1st again if that is where an 18 hole match had started) and would continue to play extra holes until one player won a hole ('sudden death').

As David pointed out, Matchplay was the more common form of amateur golf, especially for the type of friendly game that they would be playing that evening. However, he couldn't resist showing off a little by telling John that when he had played some golf in Florida last year with an American friend, he'd noticed that even casual matches there often took the form of Strokeplay.

John was still slightly puzzled: why was virtually all the golf he saw on TV Strokeplay when most amateur golf was Matchplay? Well, as David pointed out, Strokeplay was obviously much simpler: the player who completes the stipulated round or rounds in the fewest strokes is the winner! Professional golfers also feel that this is a fairer test of their ability, less subject to the vagaries of fortune in hole-by-hole Matchplay. It was also easy to administer, knowing how long the competition would last, i.e. 72 holes. The trouble with Matchplay was that you never knew whether it would end early or go into extra holes.

HANDICAPPING

However, amateurs do play Strokeplay for one very important reason: for handicap purposes. The club Medal (Strokeplay) competition is the usual way of assessing a player's handicap against a 'Standard Scratch Score (SSS)' which is nowadays a computed figure for the day of the competition in question. But handicapping schemes are not part of the Rules as such and do vary around the world.

Which left the question of a handicap for John for this evening's match. David suggested that, from what he had seen of John's swing at the driving range, he would give him an unofficial handicap of 24 (the maximum men's handicap is 28). So the difference between their two handicaps would be 13 strokes and David explained that in Single's Matchplay, John would receive three quarters of the difference (9.75), rounded up to 10 strokes. Naturally, as they were just playing 9 holes, John would in fact only get 5 strokes. At which holes would John get the strokes? Simple, said David, at the first 5 of the stroke index holes 1 to 10 as shown in the stroke index column on the card.

STROKE INDEX

John had to admit that he found the numbering in the stroke index column pretty baffling. David agreed that a clear explanation was needed and it was all to do with rating the holes in order of difficulty, with stroke 1 being the most difficult, up to stroke 18 as the easiest. The purpose of this was to indicate where handicap strokes are taken, starting with the most difficult hole, i.e. Stroke 1. So in a full 18-hole match, John would receive his 10 strokes at the 10 most difficult holes: stroke index (SI) 1 to 10. To give a fair balance throughout the 18 holes, the stroke holes are usually divided equally between the first nine and the second nine holes on the course, by odd and even numbers. David showed John on the card: S.I. holes 1,3,5,7,9,11,13,15,17 appeared on the front nine so his strokes would be at 1, 3, 5, 7, 9.

CHAPTER 2 – Playing by the rules off the 1st

Now with a decent ball in one hand and his driver in the other, John was just about ready to follow David on to the 1st tee until David announced that he was playing a Maxlop 3 ball. What an amazing coincidence: so was John! David said it was just as well that they checked, because if you can't identify your ball, it's lost (Rule 27).

So both John and David would have 'lost' their balls if they couldn't tell which was which after teeing off So David changed his ball for a Maxlop 1 and for good measure marked a couple of dots on the ball with a biro so that he would definitely know that it was his.

TEEING OFF TIPS

John stood on the tee absentmindedly jangling some coins in his pocket as David prepared to unleash his first drive (they had tossed a coin for the 'honour' or Order of Play: Rule 10-1). Suddenly, David stopped at the top of his backswing - the jangling was very distracting – and gave John a gentle reminder about one of the basic rules of Etiquette: player consideration: don't move, talk (or jangle coins!), stand too close to or directly behind a player making a stroke.

A famous professional of a former era, who shall remain nameless, was often accused of a form of gamesmanship when he shuffled his highly polished white golf shoes just within his fellow competitor's peripheral vision. Anyway John was highly embarrassed (not a good start to his membership campaign).

David also asked John to stand facing him, either level with or behind the line of the ball, rather than behind him, where he would be visible in the corner of David's eye in a distracting way during the backswing. As David said, golf was a difficult enough game without added distractions.

However, John's embarrassment quickly disappeared when by some miracle he managed to follow David's immaculate 220 yard drive down the middle with one of his own that finished on the fairway only some 20 yards behind. As they walked towards their drives, John did remember that he would be playing his next shot before David: when balls are in play, the ball furthest from the hole is played first (Rule 10-lb).

PLAY IT AS IT LIES

John's pleasure at his opening drive was short lived when he saw where his ball was lying - right in somebody's old divot mark (that certainly should have been replaced as a matter of Etiquette). As it seemed plainly unfair that he should be penalized for some other player's inconsiderate behaviour, he was just about to pick up his ball and place it in a more favourable spot when David intervened. John was soon made aware of perhaps one of the most fundamental Rules of Golf, which goes a long way to explaining the logic behind many of the other rules. Rule 13-1 simply states that "the ball shall be played as it lies, except as otherwise provided in the Rules". No mention of fairness, or other players' inconsiderate behaviour! Golf was not designed as a "fair" game, but the expression "rub of the green" will remind you that in golf you have good fortune (when you next find your ball sitting up beautifully in deep rough when you had thought it lost) as well as bad.

Playing it as it lay, John found that by hitting down hard on the ball with a 7-iron, he actually managed quite a good shot from the offending divot mark. In fact, there was a little bit of extra pleasure in hitting such a good
shot whilst adhering strictly to the rules!

An immaculate 5-iron put David in the middle of the green of the 380-yard opening hole (SI 9) and John was pretty pleased to be on in three after being in the divot. As they walked on to the green, John noticed David repairing the pitchmark where his ball had landed on the green, and dutifully did the same himself.

It hardly needs stressing that if nobody repaired their pitchmarks, the greens would soon become a mass of little craters.

TENDING THE FLAG

As he was a lot further from the flag than David, he knew it was his turn to play first, so not wishing to hold up play unduly, he prepared to putt at the flags tick, until suddenly David asked him if he would like it 'attended'. He had to admit ignorance at David's use of this strange word, but was soon put right about the various flagstick rules.

In fact, there are two basic principles to remember: if you are playing towards the flagstick from off the green, it doesn't matter if your ball hits it, but once you are on the green, it does. So as David pointed out, John was putting from on the green, so he must either have the flagstick removed or attended. If attended by David, the flagstick would be removed as John putted so that the ball didn't strike it. (Rule 17-3: penalty for striking the flagstick: Matchplay - loss of hole, Strokeplay – two strokes.)

As John's putt was about 40 feet away, he decided he would have the flagstick attended otherwise it would be quite difficult to see the hole. It was a pretty good putt, too, just three feet short. He decided to hole out straightaway and, as is required in Matchplay, politely asked David if he could continue putting even though he was closer to the hole. Being as it was a friendly match, David agreed and, before John holed out, he laid down the flagstick carefully so as not to damage the green, and well away from any danger of either of their putts hitting it .

So a one-over-par five at the first was a pretty satisfactory start for John, who stood quietly as David putted out for a regulation par and then replaced the flagstick, making sure it was properly in the hole.

CHAPTER 3 – Provisional play on the 2nd

They had halved the first with John's stroke taken into account, so the 'honour' continued with David on the 405-yard 2nd. As David teed up his ball, John was rather surprised to see him standing apparently outside the teeing ground with the tee marker between his feet and the ball!

TEEING GROUND TACTICS

Seeing the look on John's face, David explained that a player may stand outside the teeing ground to play a ball within it (Rule 11-1). But why would he want to do that, John quite reasonably asked? David gave him another useful practical tip. The teeing ground was the one area on the course where you had a choice of the place from which you could play your ball - anywhere within the definition (Rule 11): a rectangular area two club-lengths in depth, the front and sides of which are defined by the outside limits of two tee markers.

David had chosen to stand outside the teeing ground to play his ball from as near as possible to the left side of the tee so he could aim more easily away from the woods down the left of the fairway. Which is exactly what he did, with his drive finishing on the right hand side of the fairway, well away from the trouble. David had demonstrated perfectly a situation where the rules can be used to your advantage.

John was not so lucky: he was so aware of the woods after David had talked about them (a possible form of gamesmanship?), that it was almost inevitable that his drive would end up there, which it duly did - a low, vicious duck-hook scuttling into the long grass under the trees. As John prepared to trudge rather dolefully towards the woods, David suggested that he played a provisional ball from the tee.

John wanted to make sure he knew exactly what to do in this situation where he might have lost his ball (and it was a frequent occurrence at this stage of his golfing life), especially as he had noticed what a lot of time seemed to be wasted on his public course by players looking for their balls. Rule 27, as David said, was definitely one of the most important to know, since it covered those situations where a ball might be lost or out of bounds.

PROVISIONAL BALL/ FIVE-MINUTE RULE

Firstly, the provisional ball. Its purpose is quite simple: to save time. The rules allow five minutes to search for a lost ball and then you have to return under penalty of one stroke to where you played from (in this case the tee) and play another ball - which is then your third stroke, hence the expression 'three off the tee'.

But of course, the walk back, and back again, is very time-consuming, all of which can be avoided by playing a provisional ball. The procedure is laid down under Rule 27-2a and must be followed precisely.

Firstly you must inform your opponent or fellow competitor that you intend to play a provisional ball, and secondly you must do it before you go forward to search for the original ball. If you fail to do either of these things, the provisional ball then becomes the ball in play, you must add a penalty stroke and the original ball is deemed lost.

A particularly cruel example of the application of this penalty occurred in the Dunhill Cup at St Andrews in 1992. In the Ireland vs Korea match, Christy O'Connor Jnr was playing Park Nam Sin who unfortunately had very little, if any, command of English. After driving off at the notorious 17th over the 'railway sheds', Park must have thought his ball had gone out of bounds. He showed another ball to the Irishman, but without saying anything, played it from the tee.

When the players went forward to the fairway, Park discovered that his ball was just in play. Naturally, he wanted to play his original ball, but O'Connor objected, saying that Park had said nothing on the tee about putting a provisional ball in play. The fact that he had been unable to utter the correct words, let alone any words, in English, was irrelevant. Technically, the second ball was in play and the referee declared that the Korean was disqualified for playing a wrong ball under Rule 15-3.

After listening to this salutary tale, John duly informed David that he was putting a provisional ball in play. This time, at least it was straight, but hardly got airborne, and ended up just 100 yards from the tee at the beginning of the fairway (well short of the point where his first drive had dived into the rough).

As they approached John's provisional ball, David advised him that he could play another stroke with it, as the player may play a provisional ball until he reaches the place where the original ball is likely to be (Rule 27-2).
This time, David opted for the safety of a 5-iron and managed to hit a good shot well down the fairway past the point where his original ball might be found, So now they began to search for John's ball and David had a pretty good idea of where it had gone into trouble as he had watched the flight of John's ball from the tee, another common sense point of Etiquette.

CALLING THROUGH

However, even though David had got a good line on John's ball, the rough under the trees was pretty thick and it was obvious that they weren't going to find John's ball quickly, if at all. David glanced back at the tee; another match was waiting, ready to play, He told John he was going to 'call them through' as it was a basic courtesy to invite the players behind to pass as soon as it becomes apparent that the ball will not easily be found, and not to search for five minutes (the time allowed for finding a lost ball: Rule 27) before doing so.

It was just their luck that almost immediately after calling the following match through, John's ball was found, not lying too badly either. Well, now they would have to wait until the other players had gone through and were out of range, but at least they had not held up play on the course.

John decided wisely not to be too ambitious with his shot from the rough and his firmly struck 9-iron got him well back onto the fairway, from where he watched David play his second shot. With 185 yards to go to the flag, it was a full 3-iron, and John was relieved to see that David was human after all as his thinly struck shot came up well short of the green.

At last they reached the green (the hole seemed to have gone on forever) with both David and John on in three strokes. As they prepared to putt, John saw David mark the position of his ball by placing a small coin behind it, lift it and clean it. After the divot mark incident on the 1st fairway, John didn't think you could touch your ball anywhere on the course, let alone lift it up and clean it; so David explained with a quick run-down on the main putting green rules (Rule 16).

ESSENTIAL PUTTING GREEN RULES

Yes, the putting green was one place on the course where you could lift your ball while it was in play (Rule 16-lb). John already knew about repairing pitch marks, of course (David interjected that this repair work also extended to old hole plugs) but could he press down those spike marks he could see on his line to the hole? No, the line of the putt must not be touched except to remove sand and loose soil and other loose impediments by picking them up or by brushing them aside with a hand or club without pressing anything down (Rule 16-la). As David added, Rule 16-ld was also important: you can't test the surface of the green by rolling a ball or roughening or scraping the surface.

After trying to take all that information in, John made a lamentable effort at his first putt, sending it careering 15 feet past the hole. Two more putts and at last it was in the hole for a six. Still, at least David was not that much better with his one-over-par five. Nonetheless that was good enough to win the hole as John did not have a stroke on the second.

CHAPTER 3 – Out of Bounds

The 3rd was a fairly daunting Par-5: 545 yards (SI 7). Daunting to John, that is, because at the local public course there were no Par-S's at all, so this would be the first that John had played. Not only the length of the hole worried John - he could also see an out-of-bounds fence all the way down the right-hand side, ready to receive his most common shot: the dreaded slice.

The 3rd held no such terrors for David. In fact, he usually played it rather well, knowing that although it was out of range in two for all but the low-handicappers, three reasonable shots would get him home comfortably. As it was also slightly downhill, he normally used his 3wood off the tee, which he was more confident of hitting straight (especially with the out of bounds lurking) and this would get him far enough down the fairway. With these thoughts in mind, David made an easy, confident swing and hit his best tee shot so far.

SLICING OUT OF BOUNDS

All John could see in his mind's eye was the out of bounds, and lacking the experience of the sort of strategic thinking that had helped David, he took out his driver, hoping that a wild thrash would send him sailing past the trouble. The result was an enormous slice, sailing well over the out-of-bounds fence.

The procedure after this is straightforward enough. Under the important Rule 27 again, if a ball is lost out of bounds, the player shall play a ball, under penalty of one stroke, as nearly as possible at the spot from which the original ball was last played, in this case the tee.

BALL KNOCKED OFF TEE

So John teed up another ball (this time with his 3-wood at David's suggestion) but still rather unnerved by his out of bounds shot, waggled his club so vigorously at address that he knocked the ball off its tee. John could hardly bear it: was this another penalty stroke? Luckily not. Under Rule 11-3, it may be re-teed without penalty. With a sigh of relief, John at last made a reasonable swing and dispatched the ball (his third shot, of course) onto the fairway.

A FREE DROP

When he reached his ball, it was embedded in the fairway right where it had landed, in its own pitchmark. After his experience with the divot mark, John thought he would have to try and play the ball as it lay and he was just preparing to have a hack at it with his wedge when David came over.

No need to play it like that: John was entitled to lift, clean and drop his ball without penalty, as near as possible to the spot where it lay but not nearer the hole. But as David added, Rule 25-2 only applied in a closely mown area, meaning any area of the course, including paths through the rough, cut to fairway height or less.

After two more shots, John was just short of the green, while David had duly managed to get on comfortably in three. John sized up his next shot: a delicate pitch off a tight lie over a bunker to a tight pin position - not a shot to be relished even by a good player and certainly not by John. A nervous prod led to the inevitable result: his ball landed in the bunker.

ON HAZARDOUS GROUND

As he stepped into the cavernous bunker, John was not feeling very confident, but at least he knew the most important rule that he must not break under penalty of two strokes: touching the ground in a hazard (whether a bunker or a water hazard) with a club (Rule 13-4). So carefully hovering his sand-wedge above the sand, he made a backswing that correctly avoided striking the sand on the way back, came down steeply into the sand behind the ball and, 10 and behold, it popped out onto the green!

RAKING THE BUNKER

Wondering why he had been so nervous in the first place, he carefully raked over his footprints (Etiquette: care of the course) and stepped on to the green to hole out in two more strokes. That meant a horrendous nine on his card, though, against David's steady par five - and not even his stroke could save him from losing this hole.

CHAPTER 5 – Water

A Par-3 over water is usually a challenging proposition and the 192-yard 4th was no exception. It was not David's favourite hole, especially if he was a little nervous in the monthly medal. But in this evening's friendly game, he felt confident with his 5-wood and his shot cleared the water easily, and although it caught the cunningly placed bunker just right of the green, he was happy enough.

Still reeling after his nine, John had very little confidence about clearing the water. But still, he had to have a try at least and thought that his best 3-wood might just carry the hazard. An almighty swish and both players watched as the ball flew towards the target (a bit low, David thought, but it might just get over). It only fell three feet short, but the splash was clear enough.

Sunk without trace.

Before they walked off the tee, David explained the important aspects of Rule 26 relating to water hazards, one of the most common trouble situations that all golfers get into. As John's ball was obviously lost in the hazard, the first point to note is that he could play another ball from the tee with the stroke and distance penalty that is always available to a player who wishes to replay a shot.

WATER HAZARD PROCEDURE

However, in the case of a water hazard, there is a less drastic option. You can proceed to the edge of the water hazard and then drop a ball behind it, keeping the point at which the original ball last crossed the margin of the water hazard directly between the hole and the spot on which the ball is dropped -

with no limit as to how far behind the water hazard the ball may be dropped (Rule 26-1b).

John was quite happy with the second option, and he dropped about 30 yards behind the water so that he could play a full sand wedge shot of 50 yards - much easier than trying a delicate 20 yard shot from the edge of the water. So, on the green in three and a chance to hole a 30-foot putt for a four.

BALL DAMAGE

Meanwhile, David was surveying his bunker shot: right under the back lip. He decided to come out sideways and duly played his ball just onto the edge, some 40 feet from the flag. As he picked up his ball to clean it, he noticed that the cover was now cut, probably as a result of his bunker shot. He called John over to show him, explaining that under Rule 5-3, he could substitute a ball if it is visibly cut, cracked or out of shape, but before lifting the ball, you must announce your intention to your opponent or fellow-competitor.

But even with a brand new ball, his putt came up ten feet short. Now it was John's turn to putt. He couldn't believe his luck when it curled into the hole with its last roll. Neither could David, whose ten footer for a half now felt a lot longer. Almost inevitably, he pulled it left of the hole.

CHAPTER 6 - The Long 5th - The Long Search

As they walked towards the 5th tee, John could hardly contain himself - after going in the water, not only had he made a four that included a penalty shot, but he had won the hole and was now only one down in the match! Coming straight after his nightmare nine at the previous hole this reversal in fortune had filled him with new-found confidence as he surveyed the 474-yard 5th.

PRACTISING - THE RULES

As he prepared to tee off, he noticed that David was practising his putting on the edge of the tee (no doubt to try and eliminate the fault that caused the pulled putt on the last green) and cheerily asked him if such practice was against the rules. Not at all, David answered confidently, because he knew the rules quite clearly on this subject after the same situation had occurred in the last monthly medal. In between holes, you may practise putting or chipping on or near the putting green of the hole last played or the teeing ground of the next hole to be played (Rule 7-2).

However, you couldn't do this anywhere else on the course, David added. For example, if you are waiting in the middle of a fairway for the green ahead to clear, you can't drop a ball and start practising you're putting or chipping. Of course, you can make practice swings anywhere as they are not strokes, although Etiquette dictates that you must not take divots when practice swinging on the tee. John asked what would happen if he found an old ball somewhere on the course and decided to whack it away over the fence - was this a practice stroke? Yes, it was and you would incur a penalty of two strokes in Strokeplay or loss of the hole in Matchplay.

As he surveyed the fairway from the elevated tee, John realized that the 5th was obviously one of the most difficult holes on the course. Apart from its sheer length, there was sharp dog-leg left nearly 220 yards from the tee, woods on the left and plenty of dense looking rough. David pointed out that on the card of the course it was indeed rated as the most difficult hole, as shown in the stroke index column: Stroke I.

John's drive hit the fairway well short of the dog-leg, but safely in play. David hit one of his longer drives which got him nicely to the corner of the dog-leg, so he would see the green when he played his next shot.

A dilemma faced John for his next shot. Should he play safe and just hit a mid-iron up to the corner of the dog-leg or should he go for a daring shot over the trees to cut off the dog-leg and gain a lot more distance? If he'd thought about it carefully, he would certainly have gone for the first option as David was giving him a stroke. But an inflated idea of his ability to hit a high draw over trees got the better of him (as it does with most golfers in this sort of situation!).

Having selected a 5-wood, he hit his second shot, which at first looked promising as it flew up towards the trees - but no, it was just too low, clipped the top of the tallest pine and crashed down into the undergrowth.

Having learned one lesson from earlier in the round, John immediately called across to David that he would put a provisional ball into play and did what he should have done in the first place - hit a safe 6-iron up to the corner of the dog-leg. David came across to help John search for the ball in the trees, an exercise fraught with possible brushes with the rules.

ROUGH JUSTICE

The rough was pretty deep where John's ball had disappeared and as they began to search, David warned John to be careful that he didn't move his ball, even accidentally, during the search because that would incur a one stroke penalty (Rule 18-2). However, if David moved John's ball, as his opponent in Matchplay (or fellow-competitor in Strokeplay), there would be no penalty (Rule 18-3,4). So John began to tread a little more carefully and stopped swishing his club at random through the rough. Within a minute, David called out that he had come across a ball.

WHOSE BALL IS IT ANYWAY?

The first thing to establish was whether it was John's ball. As they had discussed on the 1st tee, John knew he was playing a Maxlop 3, but the trouble was he couldn't see enough of the ball in the rough to identify it as his, especially as it was quite muddy as well.

But under Rule 12-2, this situation is covered (if you'll pardon the pun): the player may, without penalty, lift a ball he believes to be his own for the purpose of identification and clean it to the extent necessary for identification. But as David added, it was also part of the rule that before lifting the ball, the player must announce his intention to his opponent in Matchplay, or a fellow competitor in Strokeplay, and mark the position of his ball. He must then give David the opportunity of observing the lifting and replacement.

John followed the procedure to the letter of the law, cleaning off just enough mud to see that it was indeed his ball and carefully replacing it in the same position before hacking it out onto the fairway with his pitching-wedge. David could just see round the dog-leg - his drive hadn't been quite as long as he would have liked - but he knew he would be pushed to get up in two. He hit the 3-wood well enough but was still 30 yards short of the green.

John thought he would have a crack with the 3-wood as well, but he hadn't played golf long enough to realize that this type of shot was pretty difficult for an inexperienced player as there isn't much loft on a 3-wood to get the ball in the air.

The result was a horrible low, banana slice which went scuttling off up the right-hand side of the fairway, only to end up in a gorse bush, still 75 yards short of the green and looking pretty unplayable.

UNPLAYABLE BALL

Rule 28 (ball unplayable) is certainly one of the most important rules as it is such a common occurrence. The key point to remember is that the player may declare his ball unplayable at any place on the course (except when the ball is in a water hazard). The player is the sole judge as to whether his ball is unplayable.

Unplayable it certainly was. It was quite visible in the middle of the gorse bush, but there was no way John could hit it. David explained the three options, all under penalty of one stroke. Firstly, he could go back to where he had hit his last shot and play again from there (Rule 20-5). Secondly, he could drop a ball within two club-lengths of where the ball lay, but not nearer the hole, or thirdly drop a ball behind the point where the ball lay, keeping that point directly between the hole and the spot on which the ball is dropped, with no limit as to how far behind that point the ball may be dropped.

The gorse bush was only about four feet in diameter, so John was able to select a spot where he could swing unimpeded by the bush, within two club-lengths of where the ball had been, and not nearer the hole. Before John dropped the ball, David explained that even this simple operation was subject to the rules. Rule 20-2 covers the procedure in some detail, which if not followed, incurs a one stroke penalty. John watched as David gave a comprehensive demonstration of the correct way to do it.

HOW AND WHERE TO DROP THE BALL

David stood erect, with the ball at shoulder height and arm's length. The ball dropped, but shot forward off a tuft of grass, ending up nearer the hole. Was this a bit of good fortune, John asked? Unfortunately not, replied David. You had to re-drop, without penalty (Rule 20-2c) which you would also do if, taking relief from an immovable or abnormal ground condition, the ball rolled back into trouble; or if the ball comes to rest more than two club-lengths from the point where it first struck the ground. If any of these things happened twice, you placed the ball as near as possible to the spot where it hit the ground when you dropped it the second time.

With the multitude of procedures now firmly entrenched in his mind, John proceeded to drop the ball and as it came to rest not further than two club-lengths away and not nearer the hole, no further action was needed - except for John to try and get on the green with his next shot! In fact, John pulled off his best little pitch of the day, with the ball ending up just 15 feet from the flagstick.
David's 30-yard chip and run looked perfect as it headed towards the hole, but neither player had noticed that John's ball lay very much on David's line of approach - bang - David's ball hit John's, sending it scuttling 10 feet nearer the hole. John thought it was his lucky day at last: now he only had a five-foot putt!

Unfortunately, it was not. Under Rule 18-5 (Ball at rest moved), if a ball in play and at rest is moved by another ball in motion after a stroke, the moved ball shall be replaced as near as possible to its original spot. That took care of john's ball, but what about David's? His ball came under a different rule in this situation: Rule 19 (Ball in motion deflected or stopped). Under sub-section 5, if a player's ball in motion after a stroke is deflected or stopped by a ball at rest, the player shall play his ball as it lies. There was no penalty for either player, but as David added, if his ball had been played from on the green, as opposed to from off it, then he would have incurred a two stroke penalty for hitting John's ball.

So John duly replaced his ball and his day was made after all: his 15-foot putt went straight into the back of the hole for a six (pretty good, considering it had included a penalty stroke) and when David took two putts for his one-over-par five, John had ended up halving the hole with his stroke taken into account.

CHAPTER 7 – Into the Wind on the 6th

The 404-yard 6th (SI 5) was usually a fairly straightforward hole as it was generally played with the prevailing wind, but this evening, an unusual breeze had sprung up in completely the opposite direction, making the hole play a lot longer than usual. It was still John's honour and he hit what he thought was a pretty good drive, only to see it barely reach the fairway as it flew up too high straight into the wind.

David was experienced enough to try and keep his drive low into the wind and succeeded moderately well in keeping the ball down with a short, punchy swing, sending it a full 40 yards past John's.

THERE'S NO SUCH THING AS AN INNOCENT QUESTION

When John reached his ball, he quite innocently asked David what club he thought he should play to keep his next shot low into the breeze. Imagine his surprise when David's reply was that John had lost the hole because he had just breached Rule 8(1): a player may ask for advice only from his partner or either of their caddies (and the opposite side of the coin is that a player shall not give advice to anyone in the competition except his partner).

A famous example of the dire consequences of the breach of Rule 8 occurred in the 1971 Ryder Cup match at St Louis between the United States and Great Britain and Ireland. In the four ball series on the second day, Arnold Palmer and Gardner Dickinson were playing against Bernard Gallacher and Peter Oosterhuis. Arnie teed off first at the 208-yard par-3 7th hole, hitting a majestic shot onto the green. The caddies for the match were college students and in a moment of overexcitement of being in the presence of his golfing hero, Bernard Gallacher's caddie asked Palmer what club he had used.

"Heck! It looked to be only a mid-iron ... " he commented. Palmer replied, ", .. 5-iron". Even though Gallacher did not hear the whispered exchange, the referee did and instantly recognized a breach of Rule 8, in the asking of advice from anyone other than your own partner or either of your caddies. The British pair lost the hole and went on to eventually lose the match 5 and 4.

Another famous example illustrates the other side of the rule: the giving of advice. In 1980, Tom Watson was playing in the last round of the Tournament of Champions, paired with Lee Trevino. Watson noticed a little flaw in Trevino's swing and casually told him about it. The TV commentator at the time noted it as a friendly gesture between two tournament players, but viewers rang the club to point out that advice was being given, contrary to Rule 8.

After the round, Watson was asked whether he had given Trevino advice and a reply in the affirmative landed him with a 2 stroke penalty. Luckily Watson had a 3 stroke lead so he still won the tournament.

John was pretty downcast after listening to David recounting these stories, thinking he had lost the hole after only playing one shot - how valuable a knowledge of the rules would have been. His train of thought was interrupted by David. It was only a friendly game this evening, after all, so David had no intention of claiming the hole there and then.

Suitably relieved, John prepared for his next shot. He certainly couldn't get up in two, but he had a stroke, so he might as well use it. He remembered how high his 5 wood went, so that certainly wasn't the club for this shot into the wind. A 4-iron should keep the ball lower and he could get on the green with his next shot. Working out the shot clearly in advance helped him make a nice smooth swing, sending the ball well up the fairway.

PERFECT TOUCHDOWN - WRONG BASE

Seeing the result of John's shot, and knowing he was giving a stroke on this hole, David really had no option but to go for the green. He struck his 3-wood shot solidly; nice and low under the wind, running 40 yards on landing, up onto the middle of the green. The only problem was that it wasn't the 6th green it ran onto; it was the 15th, just 30 yards to the right of the 6th green.

When John reached his ball in the middle of the fairway, he almost couldn't find it. No wonder: they found it after a minute or two half-way down a rabbit hole. There was quite a plague of rabbits on the course, David explained, but not to worry, he didn't have to play it as it lay, as the situation was specifically covered by Rule 25-1: interference by a hole, cast or runway made by a burrowing animal, a reptile or a bird. So John would get a free drop within one club-length of the point that avoided the condition, not nearer the hole.

TO DROP AGAIN?

As John dropped his ball away from the rabbit holes, he was trying to remember all the correct procedures from the 5th and when the ball landed and rolled another couple of feet away from the one club-length point, he thought he had better pick the ball up and drop it again. David stopped him just in time. If John had picked up his ball, he would have been penalized two strokes, as it was now in play because it had not rolled more than two club-lengths away from the point where it hit the ground.

THE SPIRIT OR THE LETTER OF THE RULES?

A famous example of a player trying to be too scrupulous in this situation occurred in the 1973 British Open at Troon. Tony Jacklin's ball had landed in a rabbit hole and he proceeded to drop without penalty two club-lengths clear of the nearest point of relief (then you were allowed two rather than one club-lengths relief).

Upon dropping, the ball rolled a few feet further from the rabbit hole and into a much better lie. Jacklin felt this fortunate roll was giving him an unfair advantage so he re-dropped in a spirit of fair play. But of course he was in breach of the rules because, just as in John's situation, his ball had not rolled more than two club lengths further away. The resulting two shot penalty possibly cost him the Open. So the lesson is to always play to the letter of the law, and sometimes it can be to your advantage.

From his good lie, John hit another superb 5-iron (it was rapidly becoming his favourite club), right onto the green. As they walked up the fairway, John wondered how David would play his ball from the 'wrong' green - the 15th. Surely he might damage the green? Yes, he might, and this is where Rule 25-3 comes into effect: you must not play the ball, but drop it, without penalty, within one club-length of the nearest point off the green, not nearer the hole.

So David dropped behind the 15th green and played a perfect, delicate little pitch to within three feet of the hole. Well, John still had a chance to win the hole with his first putt, but he came up three feet short. The two players looked at each other - yes, a friendly half was agreed, so they picked up their balls and moved on to the 7th hole.

CHAPTER 8 – 7th Heaven

The second par-3 on the front nine was simply a delightful looking hole, played from an elevated tee, with a stream meandering up the left-hand side, only ten yards or so from the side of the green at one point, which itself was ringed with a necklace of bunkers. The 7th only measured 152 yards and David couldn't wait to hit his tee shot as he could usually rely on a steady par three at his favourite hole.

Having selected a 6-iron, David made a confident swing, perhaps a little over-confident, and although he struck the ball well, there was just a hint of a pull, but unfortunately that was enough to send the ball into the stream on the left, just short of the green. David couldn't remember the last time he had been in that stream.

John had also been expecting to see David's ball land safely in the middle of the green and having been standing rather dejectedly on the side of the tee, suddenly found himself with a chance to get back in the match. Could he pull off a reasonable shot? John thought carefully: a steady 5-iron should do the trick and he swung back nice and slowly, trying not to rush the swing as he usually did. The ball flew straight as an arrow onto the middle of the green. Advantage John!

ASSISTED PASSAGE

As John and David walked down towards the 7th green, an extraordinary thing happened. A large bird – it happened so quickly they couldn't make out the species and there were some very big birds nesting in the woods around the course, swooped down, picked up John's ball and dropped it in the stream as it flew off - very near to the watery grave where David's ball lay.

Both players looked at each other in disbelief and John was immediately concerned that the rules would once again conspire against him to deprive him of his good tee shot. Not at all, said David. There are many instances where the rules help rather than hinder and this was certainly one of them.

WHAT IS AN OUTSIDE AGENCY?

The situation is covered under Rule 18: ball at rest moved and in this case by an 'outside agency' (18-1), which is defined as any agency not part of the match, or in Strokeplay, not part of the competitor's side, and includes a referee, marker or observer or a forecaddie. Wind or water are not outside agencies, but animals carrying off your ball certainly are. Dogs and crows are particularly partial to golf balls, and in a well documented instance, a plague of crows on the Royal Liverpool course at Hoylake stole 26 in one day, selecting only new balls. The ball is replaced without penalty, or another one substituted if it has been carried off for good.

A highly relieved John picked his ball out of the stream and replaced it on the green, as near as possible to where he estimated the ball had been, and returned to the stream to see what rulings might be involved for David (for a change!) in extricating himself from trouble. The first thing he noticed was that there were red posts either side of the stream and he asked David if that was significant. It certainly was, David replied, as it denoted a lateral water hazard, rather than just a water hazard such as John had been in on the 4th, which are marked by yellow posts.

A WATER SPORT?

David considered his options. He could see the ball quite clearly as the stream was only a few inches deep and his first thought was that he might attempt to play it from the water. However, this is never as easy as it looks especially as there is refraction in the water so the ball is never quite where it appears to be.

A classic example was demonstrated by the American player Payne Stewart, playing against Jose Maria Olazabal, in the 1989 Ryder Cup at The Belfry trying to play out of the edge of the infamous lake at the 18th. Although he could see the ball reasonably well, he could only get it out a few feet at his third attempt.

Moreover, you have to make sure you do not touch the water before your stroke or in the backswing - exactly the same rule applies as in a bunker - as the first ever Swede to play in the US Masters, Anders Forsbrand, found to his cost in the 1993 Championship. His second shot on the par-5 13th finished in the notorious Rae's Creek in front of the green, and he seemed to have made a miraculous five after he played
out of the water and was down in two putts.

However, an official spotted that he 'grounded' his club in the water before he played the shot, so he incurred a two stroke penalty (Rule 13-4): total seven. Incidentally, if he had grounded his club in the water to prevent himself falling, there would have been no penalty (13-4.1).

OPTIONS OUT OF THE WATER

All in all, it did not seem such a good idea to play the ball as it lay - and he'd certainly get rather wet if he did. That left three options, all under penalty of one stroke. Firstly, he could go back to the tee and play another ball, secondly he could drop a ball on the extension of a line between the hole and the point at which the ball last crossed the margin of the hazard (as John had already done on the 4th).

The third option applies only to lateral water hazards and this looked like David's best bet: he could drop a ball outside the water hazard within two club-lengths of the point where the original ball last crossed the margin of the water hazard or a point on the opposite margin of the water hazard equidistant from the hole (Rule 26-1c).

David decided to take full advantage of this last possibility and drop on the far side (to the left) of the stream. The reason was simple. If he dropped on the right, he would not have to play over the stream. But he would have a very large bunker between him and the green however.

By dropping on the left, it was true that he would have to play over the stream, but he would have a clear line to the flag through the one decent gap in the necklace of bunkers. This was definitely the 'percentage' shot and David played a confident little pitch to put himself just ten feet from the flag.

But John was still in the driving seat, just 25 feet from the flag. All he needed to do was take two putts for his par three and he would win the hole, even without a stroke, because David had already played three with his penalty stroke added. John steadied himself - no need to rush at the putt and end up charging it ten feet past – just a gentle push towards the hole to leave a 'gimme'. He made a good stroke and his ball ended up right on the edge of the hole - in fact, John couldn't believe that the ball wasn't going to drop in. He made his way to the hole and stood there waiting for the ball to drop.

WILLING THE BALL IN

After half a minute, the ball fell in the hole: a birdie two! Or so John thought until David pointed out that Rule 16-2 only allowed the player enough time to reach the hole without unreasonable delay and then a further ten seconds to determine whether the ball is at rest.

David said the rule was quite clear because he had seen exactly the same thing happen to Sam Torrance on TV in the 1991 English Open on the spectacular par 4 10th at The Belfry. John was astonished: was he going to be penalized and lose the hole after all? Yes and no, luckily in that order for John. He had to add a penalty stroke to his score, but the player is deemed to have holed out with his last stroke, so John still ended up with his par three. The hole was won after all and now John was all square with just two to play.

CHAPTER 9 – Rain at the 8th

When they had set out from the 1st just an hour and a half ago, it had been a beautiful summer's evening, but suddenly a couple of enormous black clouds were racing towards them. David said he had heard something about thundery showers on the weather forecast (after farmers, golfers are the most obsessed category of weather forecast listeners), so he had come prepared with his waterproofs.

Actually, so had John, as he had just bought some to complete his golfing wardrobe. As the first large drops of rain began to fall, they quickly donned their protective layers and John started to scamper for the nearest shelter. David said they should not shelter unless there was danger from lightning - bad weather alone is not a sufficient reason for discontinuance of play: (Rule 6-8).

After all, what were their waterproofs for!

WRONG TEEING GROUND

So they were soon on the 8th tee, which was in fact a large double tee which was also for the 16th. It was John's honour, of course, and as he stepped onto the tee in the heavy rain, his greatest concern was trying to keep himself and his equipment reasonably dry. What he didn't notice was that he was in fact teeing up between the markers for the 16th.

David was pretty distracted with trying to keep the grip of his driver dry and now, just too late, he saw what John was about to do: play from the wrong teeing ground. John's club swung down and away went the ball – a terrible drive that dribbled along the ground for no more than 100 yards, nestling down in the rough well short of the fairway at this 425-yard hole (SI 3). As John bent down to retrieve his tee peg, he realized to his horror just what he had done. He felt instinctively that the rules were probably going to cruelly deprive him of the hole.

But no, in this case the rules are not too unkind, at least in Matchplay. Rule 11-5 states that it is the opponent's prerogative as to whether the player has to cancel the stroke and play another (with no penalty), or let the original tee shot stand which, if it were a poor one, would be in David's favour. (In Strokeplay, however, there is a two stroke penalty and the shot must be replayed from the teeing ground.)

So it was up to David whether he would make John play his tee shot again. Here was an opportunity to be kind or cruel to his golfing partner. To make him play again would be kind as it gave John a chance to hit a better tee shot (hopefully he couldn't hit a worse one). To make him play his dreadful tee shot from out of the rough would be quite cruel.

A SPORTING GESTURE

David decided very quickly that the kind option would be a good sporting gesture to his new golfing friend, so he explained the situation to John and asked him to replay his tee shot. A duly grateful John, given a second bite of the cherry, produced one of his best shots of the day, a really satisfying drive of at least 220 yards, ending up just on the right-hand side of the fairway.

CASUAL WATER

With John receiving a stroke on this hole, David now had his work cut out. But he also hit a good drive, just a few yards ahead of John. As they walked briskly after their drives, the rain was pounding down hard on their umbrellas, with puddles beginning to form everywhere on the fairway ahead.

In fact, when they reached John's ball, it was right in the middle of a small pool of water. Surely John didn't have to play it from there? No, he certainly didn't have to, said David, because under Rule 25-1, he was entitled to relief, without penalty, from 'casual water'.

The definition of casual water is important: a temporary accumulation of water on the course which is visible before or after the player takes his stance and is not in a water hazard. This casual water was obviously visible before John took his stance, but David explained that if in another situation water welled up around John's shoes as he took up his stance on what seemed to be dry ground, this would also be casual water (although a Local Rule may be made denying a player relief from interference with his stance).

The relief procedure has to be followed to the letter. It has to be the nearest point of relief which (a) is not nearer the hole, (b) avoids interference by the condition, and (c) is not in a hazard or on a putting green. The ball is then dropped within one club-length of this point.

SEMI-ROUGH LUCK

When John looked at his ball, it was clearly nearer the far side of the puddle, but that would mean if he dropped it on that side, it would be off the fairway in the semi rough. Surely that was unfair, because as his ball was after all lying in a puddle on the fairway, shouldn't he be allowed to drop it on the fairway? Unfortunately not, said David, it had to be the nearest point of relief. So there was no alternative for John but to drop in the semi-rough (he could have played the ball as it lay, of course), and his drop put him in a very fluffy lie. Hardly a fair deal.

Still, he had to accept the situation and get on with it, and he reckoned that the safest course of action would be a 7-iron to get back onto the fairway, especially as his best shot with a longer club would not be enough to reach the green however well he hit it. (He was now learning by his earlier mistakes how to think his way round the course.)

'I DIDN'T TOUCH THE BALL!!'

Just as he drew back the 7-iron, he couldn't believe his eyes when the ball moved, rolling back a full inch. At first, he was tempted to carry on and try and hit it, but he stopped and told David what had happened, saying that he hadn't touched the ball before he started his backswing, so surely there was no penalty.

David felt this was as good a time as any to explain the whole situation about a ball at rest moved by a player (Rule 18-2) as it was an important rule and one that was frequently misunderstood.

Luckily, there was nobody pressing behind them, so David was able to take John slowly through the vital points. Firstly, there is the general point that if you cause the ball to move, you incur a penalty stroke, and the ball is replaced. Bearing that in mind, what is the definition of 'caused'? As John had said, he hadn't actually touched the ball.

THE RIGHT 'ADDRESS'

He may not have touched it, but a penalty stroke was incurred because the ball moved after he had addressed it - 'addressed' meaning that you have put your feet in place for the stroke and grounded the club. Had John done both of these things, David asked? Yes, he had. David pointed out that many good players hover the clubhead above the ground if they think the ball might move, because that reduces the chances of the ball being nudged by the clubhead, or by the grass as the clubhead settles into it.

BALL DEEMED TO HAVE MOVED

This actually means that the ball leaves its position and comes to rest in any other place (fig 11a) (even if only by a fraction). If the ball just rocks slightly, which can often happen in strong wind, and then settles back in the same position, then there is no penalty (fig 11b). The whole subject of the ball moving at address is very much part of the 'self-policing' nature of the rules of golf; basically it is up to the individual player's conscience.

There was another match approaching the tee behind them now, so it was time to get on with the game. There was still a lot of golf to be played on this 8th hole. So John duly replaced his ball under penalty of one stroke, but at least he hit a good 7-iron well up the fairway. David thought he was in a pretty good position on this hole now. John had played three (nett two, with his stroke) but was still well short of the green.

One good shot and he could wrap up the hole. He would need a 3wood as the ground was now pretty wet and he wouldn't get much run on the ball, but he should make the green alright. But in reality, he was asking a lot in the wet conditions, and trying to swing that extra bit hard, he came right 'over the top' and pulled th- shot under the trees, short and left of the green. So much for the hole-winning shot!

John had also been thinking that the end of the 8th was nigh but now, seeing David's ball disappear under the trees, he realized that all was not yet lost. A good iron shot and he could be back in the hole. John reckoned the middle of the green was about 160 yards away, perhaps a 5-iron; but having seen David's problems trying to hit flat out in the wet conditions, he thought an easy 4-iron was a better proposition. It certainly was, because although he slightly mishit the ball, the 4-iron still had enough run on it to trundle onto the green.

David was in a horrible spot. Right under the low branches of the pine trees, with pine cones and pine needles everywhere. As he made his way gingerly under the branches (and they were dripping wet too), he called John over. Here was an ideal place to tell John about the final aspect of Rule 18-2(c): a ball moving after any loose impediment lying within a club-length of it has been touched by a player.

NATURAL IMPEDIMENTS TO NATURAL PLAY

John's first question was what on earth were loose impediments? Yes, it was vital to know the definition, replied David. They are natural objects such as stones, leaves, twigs, branches and the like, dung, worms and insects and casts or heaps made by them, provided they are not fixed or growing, and are not solidly embedded or adhering to the ball.

David emphasized that the important word was 'natural', so it would include such things as banana skins and even dead rats! It certainly included the pine cones and needles around David's ball, so he approached it very carefully, because if his ball moved while he was touching these loose impediments within one club-length of his ball, he would incur a one stroke penalty.

ON YOUR KNEES

Trying to manoeuvre himself carefully into position, David realized that the only way he was going to be able to hit the ball was on his knees and the ground was soaking. It would be nice to kneel on something, he mused, until he remembered the incident involving the American tournament player Craig Stadler. In a similar situation to David's, he had knelt on a towel to play his shot from under the trees. The incident was reported and Stadler was held to have breached Rule 13-3, whereby a player is entitled to place his feet firmly in taking his stance, but he shall not build a stance. The unfortunate Stadler was penalized two strokes.

So David decided he would just have to suffer wet knees, and from his unconventional stance was only able to hit the ball a few yards under the branches, ending up still not quite out of the woods. His next stroke was also going to present difficulties: he was hardly able to make a backswing because of the branches behind him.

MOVING, BENDING, BREAKING

John continued to watch David's trials and tribulations being on the green in four (nett three) was beginning to look quite good now. David meanwhile was trying to take up some kind of stance amongst the branches and thought he might as well inform John about the dangers of this particular situation under Rule 13-2: improving your lie, area of intended swing or line of play. In David's case, he would have to be careful not to move, bend or break anything fixed or growing, except in fairly taking up his stance or making his stroke or backswing. In other words, as he said to John, he couldn't decide to break a few branches off behind him before he played his shot, just because they were in the way of his backswing.

The branches were certainly in the way. He tried desperately to make a half-backswing, but even this tangled up in the branches, resulting in a half-strangled stab at the ball which sent it all of four feet. Was David ever going to finish this hole!

But at least he was now just clear of the trees and was able to make a proper swing at the next shot which he put to within 12 feet of the flag. But he didn't in his heart of hearts think that would be good enough, even if he holed the putt for a six.

STILL ALL SQUARE

John's task to win the hole seemed pretty simple; get down in two putts from 25 feet. But as he crouched down over the first putt, he felt a strange sensation he hadn't experienced before in golf - nerves. Could he really hole out in two in this crucial situation? The element of doubt that had crept into his mind exerted its evil influence and sent his first putt charging six feet past.

David saw his chance to strike back, knowing he had to hole his putt for any chance to halve the hole. Using all his 20 years' experience, he steeled himself over his ball, resolved not to look up until he heard it drop in the hole and made the smoothest stroke he could muster.

The result was never in doubt - straight in the middle of the cup! Down in six!

John was stunned. Now he had to hole his six footer to win the 8th after he thought it was going to be so easy. Although lacking David's experience, there were two things about the putt he faced to make it a bit easier: it was straight and it was uphill, so he could have a good go at it without worrying about going too far past. He didn't take as much time over it as David, just lined it up quickly and banged hard. It was a good, bold putt, but just too hard - the ball hit the back of the hole and agonisingly spun out. Seven, nett six.

Still all square with one to play.

CHAPTER 10 – All on the 9th

So after all the to-ing and fro-ing, David and John's 'friendly' match was going to be decided on the 9th, a short, but treacherous looking par-4 of just 350 yards. John's strokes were all gone now, but at least the relative shortness of the hole would give him a good chance of getting on in two. From David's point of view, the 9th was deceptively easy: deceptive because he knew of the dangers lurking all the way down the hole.

NEVER RULE OUT THE HAZARDS

First of all, the drive. Too far left, and you ended up on or over the driveway to the clubhouse, or a bit further, out of bounds. Too far right, and you were in the newly planted copse of birch trees. Too far and straight, and you were in the stream that went right across the fairway only 220 yards from the tee.

The second shot wasn't much easier. The raised green presented a tiny target with severe slopes off both sides and two strategically placed bunkers at the front. In fact, David was pretty relieved that John did not have a stroke at their final hole (unfortunately for John it was stroke index 11 and he was only receiving strokes up to stroke index 10).

As John prepared to tee off on this final hole of the evening, he was mercifully unaware of the potential score-wrecking features of the 9th (which is often why you play a strange course well the first time - you don't worry about the hazards because you're not aware of them). To him, it looked a pretty straightforward drive, so he swung freely at the ball. It was a good hit, but with
a trace of a slice, just enough to send it into the edge of the new tree plantation on the right. John cursed his luck (under his breath), but David told him that he'd had a lucky break - it was

ground under repair (G.U.R.) around the new trees, as he now could see from the G.u.R. sign and the white line around the plantation.

GROUND UNDER REPAIR (G.U.R.)

Any portion of the course can be marked by order of the Committee as G.U.R. and the definition also includes material piled for removal and a hole made by a greenkeeper, even if not so marked, for example. So under Rule 25-1, John would get a free drop under the same relief procedure as for casual water, as he had done on the 8th.

The thing that worried David most was hitting his drive too far, into the stream. So, as he usually did, he took a 3-iron to lay up short of the water. But as he swung down through the ball, he made the fatal error most common to playing the lay-up shot – he subconsciously backed off hitting through properly, even though he knew that however well he hit the ball, he couldn't reach the water with a 3-iron. The result was an ugly low pull, ending up on the road to the clubhouse. Still, at least it wasn't out of bounds.

As they walked down from the tee and prepared to go their separate ways to either side of the fairway, David checked with John that he was clear what to do with his ball in the G.U.R. Yes, John was quite clear. Free drop, within one club-length of the nearest point of relief, not nearer the hole. David then added that he was also going to get a free drop from the road. Didn't he have to play it as it lay? No, because the road came under the definition of an obstruction (Rule 24).

MOVABLE/IMMOVABLE OBSTACLES

An obstruction is basically anything artificial (as opposed to something natural, which as we saw earlier, would be classed as a loose impediment) and there is a further sub definition of movable (24-1), or immovable (24-2).

Movable obstructions include non-natural things such as cans, cigarette packets, plastic bags or bottles. Not knowing that a bottle was a movable obstruction probably cost Harry Bradshaw the 1949 Open Championship. His ball came to rest against a bottle, and thinking that it was a loose impediment, he concluded that he was not allowed to move it. So he played it as it lay, bottle and all, and took six on a par-4. He subsequently tied Bobby Locke and lost in the play-off.

The road was obviously 'immovable', but John wanted to know what else might be a common example. David pointed further down the hole to the greenkeepers' shed off the right hand side of the fairway - if you were so close to it that it interfered with your stance or swing then you would get a free drop away from the obstruction at the nearest point of relief, as with G.U.R. However, David added that you wouldn't get relief just because the shed was on your line of play towards the hole: it had to be interfering with your stance or swing.

With both players clear about the relief they were going to get, they had soon dropped correctly away from their respective problem areas and were ready to play. John first. Without a stroke on the hole, he reckoned he had to go for the green, but he had a fair chance because there was only 170 yards left after his drive of about 180 yards (the slice had taken a bit of distance off it). John surveyed the shot. With the small raised green, it was not going to be easy, but one thing was sure: he would need a really high shot to carry all the trouble and get up on the green. With this in mind, he reached for his 5-wood. Even with his limited experience of golf, he knew how useful a club that could be: plenty of loft, the shaft not too long, and a much easier prospect than a long iron which was difficult to hit high.

An easy swing would do it, thought John, and he made great contact with the ball, sending it nice and high just as intended. It was straight too - John held his breath and was bitterly disappointed when he saw it plunge into the huge bunker, right on line, but just a couple of yards short of the green.

David was certainly relieved when he saw the result of John's shot. Although he didn't have to come in directly over the bunker like John, it was still a very tricky shot in terms of club selection. He only had a yard or two less than John - about 165. Should he play a 4-iron to be sure of getting there, or should he hit a high 5-iron which would have a better chance of holding on the green? After a moment or two's hesitation he decided to go for the high 5-iron.

David's shot flew high and true, but like John, he too came up short, with his ball coming to rest half way up the steep bank on the left hand front of the green. It would all be down to chipping and putting now.

As John approached the cavernous bunker, his brain was whirling. How could he get the ball high enough out of the sand to get over the huge lip and up on to the green? He stepped into the bunker only to be completely baffled. Where was his ball? He was absolutely certain it had gone straight in, but the sand was very deep and soft, so perhaps it had buried itself. He called David over who agreed he had also seen the ball go in. So what was the procedure now?

SEARCH & RE-COVER

David had to run through the possibilities that could occur under Rule 12-1 or Rule 15 - 2. First of all, searching for and identifying a ball in a hazard is different from a normal situation: in a hazard, if a ball is covered by loose impediments or sand, the player may remove by probing, raking or other means, as much thereof as will enable him to see part of the ball and there's no penalty if you accidentally move it (12-1). But you can't lift it for identification (12-2). Indeed, if you remove too much sand, you have to re-cover the ball before you play it!

So as John and David started to prod the sand with a rake, John was rather concerned about what would happen if they found a partially covered ball and John played it, only to discover that it was not his? No problem; under Rule 15-2, if a player plays any strokes in a hazard with a wrong ball, there is no penalty and the strokes do not count. Finally, John wanted to know what would happen if they didn't find it at all. Simple, said David, proceed under Rule 27 and go back to play another shot from where you played the last one under the stroke and distance penalty.

BUNKER DROP

The five minutes allowed for searching for a lost ball was nearly up when David suddenly uncovered the top of a ball in the sand. John had a good look - the brand name was visible - and it was indeed his ball, almost under the lip of the bunker and three-quarters buried! This was the one situation he hadn't thought about: his ball being unplayable in the bunker. What were his options now?

They come under Rule 28, which John had already experienced when he'd been under the bush on the 5th, and all carried a one-stroke penalty, but as David pointed out, there was one important difference. If you want to take the option of dropping on a line keeping the point where the ball lay directly between the hole and where you want to drop, you must still drop in the bunker. Otherwise drop within two club-lengths, (in the bunker, of course), not nearer the hole, or go back and play again from where you played the original shot that got you into trouble.

Well, John certainly didn't want to go right back and play such a difficult shot again, so he considered the options in the bunker.

There was a spot he could drop within two club lengths that gave him a reasonable angle to the flag, so he went for that. His drop left him not much better off, but he made a good, full swing into the sand behind the ball, sending the ball up nice and high onto the green, 20 feet from the hole. Still a chance to get down in five.

After what seemed an age helping John in the bunker, David was at last able to go back to his ball to contemplate his tricky little pitch. The problem was that the ball not only lay on a very severe slope up to the edge of the green, but was also perched precariously in the grass. David reckoned he would have to try a delicate lob with a sand-wedge.

Taking care not to dislodge the ball as he addressed it (he didn't ground the club in case the ball moved), he tried to sweep it up into the air. He got under it, alright, so much so that he actually hit it twice because the clubhead snagged in the grass as he hit the ball.

DOUBLE HIT

The distinctive double click told him that he had made a double hit. This is another classic example of golfers having to admit unilaterally that they have broken a rule (there was no way John would have known of David's infringement as he was too far away to hear anything).

David's ball landed on the green, and John was pretty surprised to then hear David call a penalty on himself. It was quite clear under Rule 14-4, David said, that if a player's club strikes the ball more than once in the course of a stroke, the player shall count the stroke and add a penalty stroke, making two strokes in all.

A famous incident of a double hit happened in the 1985 US Open at Oakland Hills, Michigan, and probably cost the unfortunate perpetrator, T.C. Chen from Taiwan, the championship. At the 6th hole in the last round, he faced just the sort of shot that David had, pitching from heavy rough at the edge of the green.

Leading the tournament at the time, the penalty stroke incurred led to a total collapse which meant that he finished second to the eventual winner, Andy North.

So the twists of fate on this last hole had put both players on the green in four strokes, and both including a penalty stroke. A five would probably win the match, but would either of them manage it?

First, David from 25 feet - just six inches short – and conceded by John. Now John, for the match. As he crouched over his putt, he had never in his wildest dreams thought that he would have a putt to win in his first game with his golfing mentor.

He put a good stroke on it and it looked all set to go in when with its last roll, it just missed the hole to the left. He hadn't seen the borrow! David generously conceded the 18-inch putt that remained, and the match was halved.

Chapter 11 – To the 19th

As they shook hands and left the green to head for a well-deserved drink in the clubhouse, John felt very pleased with his evening's work. He had taken on an experienced golfer and come out with a half. That was the beauty of golf, of course. With the handicap system, players of all different abilities can enjoy their golf together and have a chance of winning.

John was adding up his score - it looked like 50 against David's 44, with a few short putts conceded. But of course, you didn't count the score in Matchplay, as David reminded him, and it wasn't surprising that their scores were high, considering the abnormal number of brushes :with the rules!

MARKING THE SCORECARD

John just wanted to know, anyway, how would you mark your card in Strokeplay? You would exchange cards with your fellow-competitor on the 1st tee, mark each other's scores down and at the end of the round, get your card back signed by your fellow-competitor, check it, sign it yourself and hand it in. Simple! But David added that the most vital thing was that you were responsible for your own score being correct - even if your marker had put it down incorrectly.

The most famous incident of a player signing for a wrong score was in the 1968 US Masters. The popular Argentinian, Roberto de Vicenzo, had posted a last round 65 and looked certain of winning until the American Bob Goalby caught him on the last to force a play-off. Or so it seemed. But the unfortunate Vicenzo had not noticed that his playing partner and marker, Tommy Aaron, had mistakenly put him down for a four at the par-4 17th when he had, in fact, got a birdie three. But the four had to stand because Vicenzo had signed for it, so 65 became 66 and Goalby, who was playing one hole behind, came in the winner.

But back to the friendly evening game and as far as David was concerned, John had come through his first real brushes with the Rules of Golf with flying colours. Although he had rather expected to beat him, David had played golf long enough to know just how unpredictable the game was. Anyway, John was certainly good enough to take 18 holes in his stride. In fact, he suggested that two of David's fellow club members could join them to make up a four ball next week. That way, John could be well on the way to being proposed for membership.

TYPES OF PLAY

The mention of the four ball reminded John that he wasn't sure about the various forms of play (Rules 29-31).

David replied that the most common format (apart from a single which they had just played) is probably four-ball better-ball matchplay, which they were going to play next week: a team game, two against two, when you all play your own ball, but only the better-ball score of your team counts at each hole. In three-ball matchplay, three play against one another, each playing two distinct matches, or in the less common best-ball, one plays against the better ball of two or the best ball of three players.

In a foursome, two play against two, but each side only plays one ball and the partners play alternate shots.
David added that foursomes were often popular in the winter months because it was a fast game and you could keep moving and keep warm! In a threesome, one plays against two and each side plays one ball.

All this information left John with just one other question: what was a Stableford (Rule 32), something he had often heard his golfing friends mention. A very popular form of competition, David replied, in which the reckoning is made by points, hole by hole, on your nett (strokes deducted) score at each hole: one point for one over par, two points for par, three for a birdie, four for an eagle, etc. So nothing beyond one over par scores anything, in which case you can pick your ball up and move on.

As he drove out of the club car park later that evening, John could only think what a great start his membership campaign had got off to (especially after he had bought a couple of drinks at the bar). Even more important, he couldn't wait to tell his friends at the driving range every detail of the most testing nine holes of golf he'd ever played.

Now if anybody had any questions about the rules ...

CHAPTER 12 – Rules Reviewed

DELVING DEEPER INTO THE RULES

John may well have thought that he was ready to answer all the questions about the rules that his friends at the driving range might throw at him - but little did he know! The reason that he knew a lot less than he thought about the rules was twofold: firstly, he and David had not encountered a totally comprehensive selection of brushes with the rules despite all the perils and pitfalls of their nine-hole round! Secondly there are many grey areas that need to be further investigated.

In theory, many of the grey areas are covered by Rule 1-4: Points Not Covered by Rule. 'If any point in dispute is not covered by the Rules, the decision shall be made in accordance with equity,' In practice, 'equity' in terms of the Rules of Golf means an interpretation of the motives behind the framing of any rule which might apply to the situation: the result is usually a logical rather than necessarily 'fair' answer.

Many such questions or disputes are covered in an ever expanding way by the annual publication Decisions on the Rules of Golf by the R&A and the USGA. Although you certainly wouldn't want to carry this weighty volume around in your golf bag, many of the Decisions make useful and enjoyable reading and some of them could be reflected in situations that John and David might have encountered in their nine-hole match - or be faced with in some future game.

MAXIMUM 14 CLUBS

Q

When John discovered he had an extra wedge in his bag, could he have declared it out of play, but kept it in his bag rather than taking it back to the boot of his car?

A

No, because he would have started the round with more than 14 clubs. There is nothing in the Rules to permit carrying an excess club declared out of play before the round, so if John had carried it round with him he would have incurred the maximum penalty in Matchplay: loss of two holes.

TENDING THE FLAGSTICK

Q

When David is attending the flag for John's putt, what is the ruling if the knob attached to the top of the flags tick falls off as David is removing the flags tick and the knob strikes John's moving ball and deflects it?

A

Once the knob fell off, it was no longer part of the flagstick, but an outside agency. Therefore the stroke is cancelled and the ball replaced - Rule 19 1-b.

Q

Could David have attended the flagstick standing behind, rather than to the side, of the hole, or by holding it upright behind the hole, with the end of the flagstick touching the green?

A

The answer in both cases is yes. In the first case, the attendant might have to stand behind the hole to avoid standing on the line of putt of another player, and although the answer in the second case is also yes, it is not recommended because of possible damage to the putting green.

1 OVER 5 MINUTE RULE

Q
John had quite rightly played a provisional ball when he thought his original ball might be lost and was lucky enough to find it within the five-minute rule after they had called the next group through. What would have happened if he had found it after six minutes and then played it?
A
The ball was lost and therefore out of play when the five minutes had expired. Therefore, John would have been playing a 'wrong ball' and would have lost the hole in match play or incurred a two stroke penalty in strokeplay, when he would also have had to go back to the tee and put another ball in play.

Q
John had not played a provisional ball, but was simply searching for his original ball, and well before five minutes was up went back to the tee and teed up another ball. David then called out that he had found the original ball. Could John abandon the teed ball and play the original?
A
Yes. The teed ball was not in play because John had not yet made a stroke at it.

Q
If the same situation had involved John's second shot on the hole and he went back and dropped a ball in the fairway where he had played his last shot from, would the same ruling apply?
A
No, because the ball was in play once he had dropped it under Rule 20-4 and the original ball would become a lost ball.

LIFTING & MARKING

Q

When John and David reach the 2nd green, they lift and mark the positions of their balls with a small coin or marker placed behind. Could they have marked them in any other way?

A

Yes. The requirement of Rule 20-1 is only that the position of the ball shall be marked. Therefore, it can be done with a tee peg, even with a leaf (but this is inadvisable as it might be blown away!) or the toe of a putter as long as it is held in position so that the ball can be replaced on the same spot.

Q

David explained that you could remove loose impediments from the line of a putt by brushing them aside with a hand or a club. What about brushing them aside with a hat or a towel instead?

A

Absolutely not. Rule 16-1a is quite specific: only a hand or a club can be used.

RE- TEE PENALTY?

Q

On the 3rd tee, John waggles his club so vigorously that he knocks the ball off its tee. There was no penalty because the ball was not in play and he was able to re-tee it. But would he have been able to re-tee if when he took a swing at it, he just made contact with it enough to topple it off its tee but the ball still lay within the teeing ground?

A

In this case, no, because once he had made a swing at the ball, it was in play and must therefore be played as it lies. If he had put this ball back on the tee, he would have incurred a two-stroke penalty under Rule 18, or loss of hole in Matchplay.

PITCHMARK PROBLEMS

Q

John's ball was embedded in its own pitchmark on the fairway and he is able to lift, clean and drop his ball without penalty. But what would have happened if the ball had rolled back into the pitchmark after he had dropped it?

A

The ball would still be considered embedded in its own pitchmark and John would be entitled to re-drop. The same ruling would also apply if a ball lands in soft ground in a closely-mown area and spins back into its own pitchmark.

HIDDEN BUNKER HAZARDS

Q

John is in the bunker and is very careful not to touch the sand on his backswing so as not to incur a two stroke penalty. If the bunker had been full of leaves and he had to search for his ball, what rules would he have to bear in mind?

A

Firstly, he is entitled to move leaves in his search, but when he finds a ball, he is not entitled to identify it as his, because it is in hazard (however, there would be no penalty if after playing it out of the bunker, he discovered it was not his). He is only entitled to uncover part of the ball if it is buried and when he makes backswing he must not touch the leaves, otherwise he would be in breach of Rule 13-4c which prohibits a player from touching a loose impediment in a hazard before making a stroke.

Q

If John had touched a bare earth wall of the bunker in his backswing, would he be breaking the rules?

A

Yes, that would be considered touching the ground in the hazard in breach of Rule 13-4b. Two stroke penalty, or loss of hole in Matchplay.

WATER HAZARDS

Q
John's ball lands in the water hazard just short of the 4th green. What would the ruling be if John, without comment, had played another ball from the tee and then finds his original ball outside the hazard?

A
The original is lost and the second ball is in play under penalty of stroke and distance.

UNPLAYABLE BALL

Q
John his ball under a gorse bush and declares it unplayable and he proceeds quite correctly to drop within two club-lengths not nearer the hole. He could also have gone back to play again from where he played his last shot in the fairway, or dropped back as far as he liked from the bush, keeping the bush in line with the hole. But what would John's options have been if he had tried to play the ball from under the bush, failed to move the ball and then declared it unplayable?

A
The answer is almost identical but not quite! The options are the same but he could not go back to the place in the fairway where he played his 'last shot' because his last shot was in this case the mishit under the bush.

Q
What would the ruling be if, when John drops his ball, it had rolled back under the bush into the same unplayable position. Would he be entitled to redrop?

A
No, presuming the ball had been dropped correctly and had not come to rest more than two club-lengths from the point at which it struck the ground, the ball was in play when it was

dropped. So John would have to play it as it lay or declare the ball unplayable again and incur another penalty stroke.

ADVICE

Q
John had sought David's advice on club selection, only to find that he would promptly have lost the hole in anything but their friendly match. If John had simply asked how far it was to the green from the tree at the side of the fairway, then what?

A
Well, a player may ask anyone to inform him as to the distance from a permanent object such as a tree, bunker or sprinkler head to the centre of the green, because that is public knowledge. However, John could not ask David how far it was from his ball to the green, as his ball would be defined as a non-permanent object. He could only ask such advice from his caddie or partner. It is also permissible to ask factual information such as the length of a hole.

Q
Are there any situations in which you can ask an opponent or fellow-competitor what club he used?

A
Yes, it would be permitted to ask this information about a previous hole. On the 6th for example, John could have asked David what club he used for his tee shot to the 4th. Similarly, if John had played his second shot on the 6th onto the green, and David had done likewise, John would have been allowed to then ask David what club he had used.

WILDLIFE RULES OK

Q

John receives a free drop because his ball has landed in a rabbit hole. Would he have been entitled to the same relief if the hole in the fairway had been made by a dog?

A

No, because the rules are quite specific about the definition of burrowing animals. It must be an animal which makes a hole in which it may live - that certainly excludes dogs! It does include such diverse creatures as moles, ground hogs, gophers, salamanders and crawfish. 'Hole' is also very specific; if John's ball had landed in the footprint of one of the above creatures, there would be no relief without penalty as a footprint is only an irregularity of surface.

On the subject of animals, the Rules of Golf are also kind enough to allow relief where dangerous creatures are involved. For example, you would not be required to play your ball as it lay if it came to rest on a bees' nest, next to an alligator or a live rattlesnake. In Equity (Rule 1-4), the player would be permitted, without penalty, to drop a ball in the nearest spot not nearer the hole which is not dangerous.

Incidentally, the Rules of Golf definitions are so precise that a live snake is an outside agency, but a dead one is a loose impediment!

As THE CROW FLIES

Q

A good example of an outside agency, of course, was the large bird that took John's ball from off the green at the 7th. But what would have happened if the players had not been able to see where John's ball had been taken from?

A

The answer is that in equity, the ball should be dropped in an area that was neither the most, nor the least, favourable of the various areas where it was equally possible that the ball originally lay.

DOWNSTREAM, UPWIND

Q
David's ball was in the stream and he decided to take a penalty drop. But if the stream had carried his ball away before he could get there and had in fact carried it out of bounds - could he replace it where it first lay in the stream?
A
No, because water is not an outside agency and his tee shot would therefore have become out of bounds. The other side of the coin is that if the ball had landed in the stream out of bounds, but then been carried back in within the boundaries of the course, it would not be considered out of bounds.

Wind is not an outside agency either, so the same principles would apply, but in one of the more bizarre decisions, a ball blown along by the wind in a plastic bag was considered to come under the ruling of an outside agency. It was ruled that in this case, the bag, not the wind, caused the ball to move and therefore the player should drop the ball directly under the place where it originally lay in the bag.

EXERTING INFLUENCE?

Q
John's ball fell into the hole after he had waited half a minute and he incurred a penalty stroke because he was only entitled to wait ten seconds. Would the ruling be different if (a) John had jumped up and down near the hole and the ball had fallen in within ten seconds or (b)if John had stood in a position to cast a shadow, hoping that the grass on the edge of the hole would wilt, and the ball fell in within 10 seconds.
A

In the case of (a), there are two possible answers. If the ball was deemed to be still moving when John jumped, it would be ruled that he exerted influence on the ball contrary to Rule 1-2. In Matchplay, that would mean loss of hole, in Strokeplay, a penalty of two strokes. If the ball was at rest when the player jumped, it would be assumed that he caused the ball to move, and he would incur a penalty of one stroke in both Matchplay and Strokeplay under Rule 18-2a and would be required to replace the ball.

In the case of (b) it was ruled that a player is not exerting influence on the ball by casting a shadow, however deliberately, so there is no penalty.

CASUAL WATER

Q
John was entitled to a free drop away from casual water on the fairway. But what would his options be if his ball lay in a bunker completely covered by casual water? Would he be able to drop a ball behind the bunker without penalty?
A
Unfair though it may seem, he would not be able to drop behind the bunker without a one stroke penalty. His options without penalty would be restricted to dropping the ball in the bunker at the nearest place, not nearer the hole, where the depth of the casual water was least.

BALL AT REST MOVED

Q
When John caused his ball to move an inch, he incurred a penalty stroke as the movement of the ball was obvious, but what would have happened if the ball had simply sunk downwards in the grass?
A

He would still have incurred a penalty stroke because the ball had not returned to its original position. The direction of its movement up, down or sideways is immaterial.

LOOSE IMPEDIMENTS

Q
David was worried that he might move some loose impediments when he went under the low branches of the pine trees. But when exactly are they 'loose'?
A
The definition of loose impediments means not solidly embedded. For example, if a stone is partially embedded and may be picked up with ease, it is a loose impediment. If solidly embedded, it is not. If one of the trees that David was under had fallen down, it would be a loose impediment provided it was not attached to the stump.

It is even possible for loose impediments to be changed into obstructions by the rules! For example, a log (loose impediment) which has been split and had legs attached has been changed by construction into a bench (obstruction) or a piece of coal is similarly transformed when manufactured into a charcoal briquette!

IMPROVING LIE OR LINE OF PLAY

Q
On one hole it was very wet under the trees when John and David played their friendly match. The branches of the tree which interfered with David's backswing were wet also. Before playing his next stroke, David shakes the water off this branch to try and eliminate the possibility of dislodged water distracting him. Is this a breach of Rule 13-2?
A

Yes. In moving the branch David would have eliminated the distraction caused by the water and thereby improved the area of his intended swing.

Q
David was aware that he must not move, bend or break anything except in fairly taking up his stance, but what exactly does 'fairly' mean in this context?
A
The intention behind the rules is to limit the player to what is reasonably necessary to take up a stance without unduly improving the situation. He is not entitled to a normal stance, but must accommodate the situation in which the ball is found to take as normal a stance as possible. Examples of what is permitted include backing into a branch even if it breaks, and bending a branch with the hands to get under the tree to play a ball. Examples of what is not considered fairly taking up a stance include deliberately moving, bending or breaking branches to get them out of the way of the backswing, standing on a branch or hooking two branches together.

Q
John's ball came to rest in an old divot mark and he quite rightly played the ball as it lay. If his ball had come to rest just in front of a divot which was folded over but not completely detached, and it interfered with his backswing, could he replace or remove the divot before playing?
A
No. As the divot was not completely detached, it is not a loose impediment, but something fixed, so its removal or replacement would be a breach of Rule 13-2 as the lie and intended area of swing would be improved.

OBSTRUCTIONS

Q

David's ball came to rest on the road and he was entitled to relief as a road comes under the definition of an immovable obstruction (any artificially surfaced road or path, i.e. covered with concrete, gravel, wood chips, comes under this definition). What would he have done if his ball had come to rest under a car or van?

A

If the car was readily movable, it should be treated as a movable obstruction and moved. Otherwise, it would be treated as an immovable obstruction and David would be entitled to claim relief under Rule 24-2b.

Q

David mentioned to John on page 94 that the green keepers' shed was a good example of an immovable obstruction if it interfered with your stance or swing. But could you claim relief from such an obstruction if your ball was clearly unplayable for some other reason, i.e. it lies between two exposed tree roots?

A

No, if the ball is clearly unplayable due to some other condition, then you cannot claim relief due to the immovable obstruction.

STICKING TO THE RULES

Q

David had the misfortune of a double hit with his pitch shot and suffered a one stroke penalty. What would the ruling be if the ball had stuck to the clubface when he made his stroke?

A

Equity would be kind in this case, as the ball would be dropped, without penalty, as near as possible to the spot where the club was when the ball stuck to it. However, if the ball had left the clubface, gone up in the air, come down again and then stuck to the clubface (it has been known to happen!), the answer would be different. In this case, the player stopped his ball and would be in breach of Rule 19-2a (ball in motion stopped or deflected) and would suffer a two stroke penalty.

ALWAYS MORE TO LEARN

Now that we have been through just a selection of further problems that John and David might have encountered during their match, you might think that being familiar with the Rules of Golf is totally impossible! But what you must remember is that, unlike John and David's eventful 9 holes, you will probably only need to consider the Rules once or twice in any round, and quite possibly not at all.

Hopefully, the knowledge gained from our tour around the rules will help you avoid committing some cardinal sins and make you more relaxed and confident, knowing that you can have an enjoyable and fair game like millions of other golfers around the world.

Printed in Great Britain
by Amazon